W9-ASR-042

Hickory Flat Public Library
2740 East Cherokee Dr.
Canton, GA 30115

SEQUOYAH REGIONAL LIBRARY

3 8749 0027 5053 9

SODA POP

At a bottling company, cans are filled with fresh soda pop.

SODA POP

Arlene Erlbach

 Lerner Publications Company • Minneapolis

THIS BOOK IS THE PROPERTY OF
SEQUOYAH REGIONAL LIBRARY
CANTON, GEORGIA

Dedicated to my son, Matthew, and my husband, Herb — A. E.

Illustrations by Jackie Urbanovic

Words printed in **bold** are explained in the glossary on page 44.

Text copyright © 1994 by Arlene Erlbach
Illustrations copyright © 1994 by Lerner Publications Company

All rights reserved. International copyright secured. No part of this book may be reproduced or transmitted in any form or by any means, electronic or mechanical, including photocopying and recording, or by any information storage or retrieval system, without permission in writing from Lerner Publications Company, except for the inclusion of brief quotations in an acknowledged review.

Library of Congress Cataloging-in-Publication Data

Erlbach, Arlene.
    Soda pop / Arlene Erlbach.
      p. cm.—(How it's made)
    Includes index.
    Summary: Describes how the ingredients of carbonated soft drinks are made, mixed, carbonated, and bottled. Includes simple recipes for making carbonated drinks at home.
    ISBN 0-8225-2386-8 (lib. bdg.)
    1. Carbonated beverages—Juvenile literature. {1. Carbonated beverages.} I. Title. II. Series: Erlbach, Arlene. How it's made.
TP630.E75   1993
663'.62—dc20   93-20106
                                     CIP
                                      AC

Manufactured in the United States of America

1 2 3 4 5 6 – I/JR – 99 98 97 96 95 94

CONTENTS

This single factory boxes thousands of cans of soda pop each day.

1

A Sweet, Fizzy Drink

What's your favorite drink to gulp down when you're thirsty? What's the best way to wash down hamburgers or potato chips? If you're like most kids, your answer is soda pop.

More than 1 billion times a day, somebody somewhere enjoys a bubbly glass of soda pop. If each glass measured eight ounces, together they would hold enough liquid to fill more than 500 Olympic-sized swimming pools. If the glasses were placed side by side, they would circle the earth almost twice.

Other than water, soda pop is the most popular drink in the world.

Soda pop provides our bodies with much-needed liquid. But it is not a substitute for juice or milk. Added to a balanced diet, soda pop is a fun way to quench thirst.

Soda pop is made from bubbly water, sweeteners, and flavored syrups. The syrups give soda pop its special taste, whether it's root beer, grape, or any other flavor.

If you have a can or bottle of soda pop in your refrigerator, pour it into a glass. Look at the foam and the bubbles. Listen to them fizz. These bubbles are called **carbonation.** They are what gives soda pop its tingle on our tongues.

Soda pop is sometimes called a carbonated beverage. The carbonation is made by mixing ordinary water with carbon dioxide gas. This treatment takes place at a bottling company—a factory that manufactures and bottles soda pop.

Want to learn more about your favorite drink? Take a refreshing gulp and read on!

Water

All living things must have water to live. Your body needs about two quarts of water each day. About half of the water you take in comes from water in the food you eat. The rest comes from the liquids you drink. You might live for a few weeks without eating anything. But you couldn't live for more than a few days without water.

Water is the main ingredient in soda pop. Sugar-sweetened soft drinks are about 90 percent water. Diet soft drinks are about 99 percent water.

The average bottling company uses lots of water—about 250,000 gallons a day. The water is pumped through pipes from a local water supply to the bottling plant, the same way that water travels to your house.

Large pumps draw water from rivers and lakes.

The water starts at a main source, such as a river or a lake. You can't drink that water, because it contains harmful **bacteria,** or germs, that could make you sick. The water is purified, or made safe to drink, at a place called a water purification plant.

First the water passes through big screens that filter out garbage, twigs, and fish. Then the filtered water is pumped to the purification plant.

There, the water enters a huge tank called a mixing basin. Large paddles inside the mixing basin stir in chemicals, including chlorine, alum, and fluoride. Chlorine kills harmful bacteria and gets rid of bad smells. Alum picks up tiny particles of dirt. Fluoride in drinking water helps keep your teeth healthy by protecting them against decay.

MIXING BASIN   SETTLING BASIN

After the water is treated with chemicals, it goes into another huge tank called a settling basin. The water sits in the basin until any sand and dirt particles settle to the bottom. Then the particles are scraped into a sewer.

Next, the water flows through a filter made of charcoal, gravel, and sand. This filter sifts out tiny bits of dirt that did not get scraped out in the settling basin. Before the water leaves the purification plant, more chlorine is added.

The water now goes into a big underground pipe called a main. In a large city, the main has branches that lead to other mains beneath every street. These mains bring water to homes, restaurants, schools, and to factories like the bottling plant.

GRAVEL
CHARCOAL
SAND

CLEAN
WATER

FILTER

At a water treatment plant, dirty water is made good-tasting and pure.

As soon as the water arrives at the bottling plant, it's purified again. You might be thinking, it just *was* purified! But there's a very good reason for repeating the process.

Large soda pop companies have bottling plants in many states. Purification plants in different places may use slightly different chemicals to treat the water. Water might also contain certain minerals, depending on where it's from. Chemicals and minerals affect the water's taste. So the water that comes out of your faucet probably tastes different than water in another city or state.

Think of what would happen if the Fizzy Cola Plant used different-tasting water for each batch of soda pop. The company's product would not always taste the same. Customers would be disappointed with Fizzy Cola if it tasted different than they expected. They might buy a different brand of soda pop next time, and Fizzy Cola would begin to lose business.

- Every second, 790 gallons of soda pop are consumed throughout the world.

- In some parts of the United States, people call soda pop just "pop," or just "soda." In parts of New England, people call soft drinks "tonic."

Soda pop bottlers treat water a second time.

To avoid this problem, bottling companies are very careful to always use the same ingredients when making soda pop. So the bottling company repeats everything that was done at the purification plant, and it does even more. The water is treated with chemicals again to remove any taste of chlorine or minerals.

Then the water is "polished," or filtered, by a very fine screen. The holes in the screen are so tiny that you could only see them with a microscope.

Throughout the purification process, people called quality control technicians taste and test the water. They make sure that it is safe to drink and that it can be used in soda pop. They check the water in test tubes and examine it under a microscope. If they notice anything wrong with the water, it's purified another time.

By the time the water passes inspection, it is extremely pure. It's piped to the flow-mix machine, which looks like a gigantic coffee percolator with pipes coming out of each side. This is where the water is mixed with the sweetened, flavored syrup that makes soda pop taste so good.

- The original name for 7-Up was Lithiated Lemon-lime.
- The recipe for Coca-Cola is locked in a bank vault.
- Soda pop was originally marketed as a medicine. People thought it cured stomach problems and nervousness.

3
Sweeteners

The sweet taste of soda pop gives carbonated beverages their wide appeal. Most soft drinks are sugar-sweetened, but not with the kind of sugar you're familiar with. White table sugar comes from sugar beets or sugarcane. Instead of that kind, most bottling companies use corn syrup—a liquid sugar made from corn.

Corn is very plentiful in the United States. It's America's number one crop. So corn syrup is the cheapest type of sweetener to use, and it tastes good too. If you have some corn syrup at home, pour it on a spoon and take a lick. It tastes sweet, doesn't it?

Corn syrup doesn't come from the kind of corn you usually eat. The corn used for corn syrup grows on much bigger cobs. Farmers don't pick the cobs until they are dried out. Then the cobs are harvested and the kernels are removed. The kernels are sold to a corn wet milling plant.

When it reaches the wet milling plant, a truck carrying grain drives over a grate. The driver opens the hopper doors to release the corn kernels, and the kernels fall through the grate and into the wet milling plant.

A corn wet milling plant is a factory that makes corn into corn oil, corn syrup, and cornstarch. To produce corn syrup, the corn wet milling plant first makes a liquid cornstarch. Then that's made into corn syrup.

A kernel of corn has three parts: the germ, the endosperm, and the hull. The milling plant needs to separate these parts to make the different corn products. The starchy endosperm is used to make the cornstarch and corn syrup.

At the wet milling plant, the whole kernels are dumped into huge tanks of warm water called steeps. There's a tiny bit of acid, called sulfuric acid, in the water too. This mixture of water and sulfuric acid will make the corn soft so the kernels' parts can be easily separated. After a day or two, the water is drained off. Then the softened corn is crushed between two enormous metal disks. The corn now looks like white and yellow mush.

The softened corn kernels are drained before they are crushed.

The cyclone separator removes the corn germ from the rest of the kernel.

The mush is pumped into a giant funnel called a cyclone separator, which takes out the corn germ. The germ is pumped to another part of the factory to be made into oil. The hulls and the starchy endosperm also flow out of the separator. This mushy mixture is ground and crushed again, and it flows over screens. The ground-up hulls stay on top of the screens. What is left is called millstarch.

The millstarch is piped into a machine called a centrifuge. This machine whirls around fast—a lot like a washing machine does. The centrifuge separates the yellow and white particles of the millstarch. The yellow part is piped away to be made into animal food. The white part is liquid cornstarch. It looks like thin white mud.

The cornstarch is washed in a machine that looks like a giant clam. Then the liquid cornstarch is ready to be turned into corn syrup. It's piped to another part of the wet milling plant—the corn syrup refinery.

The liquid cornstarch flows into a big round tank called a column. Inside is an **enzyme,** a substance that causes a chemical change in another substance. The enzyme in this column makes the cornstarch more watery. It also begins to turn the cornstarch into sugar.

After being treated with the enzyme, the cornstarch goes into a tank to be steamed. The steaming process thins out the liquid even more. Then the liquid enters another column, where it's exposed to a second enzyme, which makes it sweet. This sweet liquid tastes like sugary water, and it's called liquid **dextrose.** In fact, dextrose is a sugar made from **starch.** The dextrose now drips through filters to get rid of any leftover corn particles. The filters also remove any strange colors, tastes, or odors.

Dextrose is a sugar, but it's not as sweet as **sucrose,** the sugar you use at home. The corn refinery now needs to make its product as sweet as sucrose. So the filtered liquid dextrose goes into another column with another enzyme. This enzyme makes the liquid very sweet. It has become a mixture of two sugars now—**fructose** and dextrose.

The fructose-dextrose mixture is filtered one last time, just as it was before. It's boiled in a tank, to evaporate any excess water. What's left is the corn syrup that sweetens your soft drink. The name for this product is high fructose corn syrup.

High fructose corn syrup is a sweet, clear liquid.

Now that the syrup is finished, the refinery pipes it into storage tanks. The syrup is also piped into trucks or railroad cars that will transport it. A truck can hold about 4,500 gallons of syrup, and a railroad car can hold about 16,000 gallons. Bottling companies buy lots of corn syrup. Some companies buy as many as six truckloads daily. And in the summer they need even more, because people are especially thirsty then and drink lots of soda pop.

The finished corn syrup is piped into a truck.

Not everyone buys sugar-sweetened drinks, though. Sugar contains lots of **calories,** the units of energy in food. If you eat many more calories than your body uses, you'll become overweight. Too much sugar is also bad for your teeth. In addition, people who have a disease called diabetes can't eat added sugar in food, because their bodies use sugar very slowly and it builds up in their blood. Sugar-free, or diet, sodas are manufactured for people who don't want sugared drinks.

Most diet drinks are sweetened with a substance called **aspartame.** Aspartame is made of two **amino acids**—phenylalanine and aspartic acid.

This white powdery sweetener is called aspartame. It is sold in the United States under the brand name NutraSweet.

- Aspartame was discovered by accident. A scientist who was studying amino acids had aspartic acid and phenylalanine on his finger. Then he licked his finger to turn a page in a book. When he tasted something very sweet, he knew he'd created an important new product.

Phenylalanine and aspartic acid are found separately in some meats, dairy products, and grains. By themselves, these amino acids don't have any taste. But when they are combined, they form aspartame. Aspartame tastes very sweet—200 times sweeter than sugar. And aspartame contains very few calories.

Another powdered chemical sweetener is **saccharin.** A few diet soft drinks are sweetened with saccharin, or with a mixture of saccharin and aspartame. Saccharin is less expensive than aspartame, but some scientists believe that saccharin causes cancer. Years ago it was tested on rats, and the rats got cancer. Even though humans would probably need to drink hundreds of glasses of soda pop each day to get cancer from saccharin, some people still don't want to use saccharin.

About 30 percent of soft drinks sold are sugar-free. About 70 percent are sugar-sweetened. Some people buy sugar-free soda pop with no artificial sweetener at all. They are a very small group, but bottlers like to please everyone.

4
Flavor and Color

Close your eyes. Think of a cold bubbly glass of soda pop. You probably have a certain flavor in mind. Is it cola, orange, or lemon-lime? Maybe it's bubble gum, apple, or watermelon. Soda pop comes in hundreds of flavors. You probably haven't heard of them all, because some flavors are sold in just a few cities.

The most popular flavors are cola and lemon-lime, followed by the Pepper-type drinks. These are caramel-colored fruit and spice blends without cola flavoring. Root beer ranks next in popularity, and orange is after that. Everything else falls in the smallest category called "all

What's your favorite flavor?

others." This group includes ginger ale, strawberry, cherry, grape, and other more unusual flavors.

To make artificial flavors, chemists analyze natural flavors to see what chemicals they are made of. Then the chemists copy them and make the artificial flavors in a laboratory.

ALL OTHERS
ORANGE
ROOT BEER
PEPPER TYPE
LEMON-LIME

COLA

Cola drinks are so popular they account for about 70 percent of all the soda pop sold. In other words, in a group of 100 people drinking soda pop, 70 would be having cola. Only about 2 or 3 would be sipping orange drinks. That might not seem like much orange. But so many people buy soda pop that those 2 or 3 people in 100 buy more than 5 million gallons of orange pop a year!

Soft drinks contain natural or artificial flavorings, or a mixture of the two. Artificial flavors are less expensive than natural flavors. Drinks like cherry, strawberry, and grape soda pop are usually artificially flavored.

Natural soda pop flavoring may contain herbs, spices, oils, or extracts. Herbs come from the leaves of plants. Spices are made from ground-up roots, seeds, and bark. Oils may come from flowers, fruits, roots, or leaves. Extracts are made by dissolving a fruit or nut in alcohol. Fruit drinks are often flavored with extracts. Drinks like lemon-lime, orange, and grapefruit are usually flavored with oils. Ginger ale and root beer are flavored with herbs and spices.

Cola flavoring is a blend of extract from the kola nut and many other flavors. It might contain cinnamon, lemon, orange, vanilla, and lime. Every company has its own recipe for cola flavor—and for any other flavor it uses. All soda pop recipes are top secret. Only a few company employees know the ingredients.

Familiar kitchen spices are used in flavoring some soft drinks. Spices in front, left to right, are nutmeg, cinnamon sticks, and ginger root.

If you have some food coloring at home, try this: Dye a glass of lemonade with orange food coloring and give it to a friend to drink. Ask your friend what it was. He or she will probably tell you it was orangeade.

Color is very important to soda pop's flavor. Color doesn't actually affect a drink's taste, but it does affect how we think about it. We expect certain colors to taste a certain way. Some orange soda actually contains more lemon flavor than orange. Lime drinks contain lots of lemon too. But you may think you are drinking orange or lime soda pop because of the drink's orange or green color. Without dye, most flavoring is either colorless or very lightly colored.

When soda pop companies buy flavorings, the color is already in them. Flavoring comes in a form called **concentrate.** Concentrate is very strong. It smells and tastes awful. It only takes a tiny bit of concentrate to flavor a bottle or can of soda pop. After water and corn syrup are added, one gallon of concentrate makes enough syrup to flavor 4,480 cans of soda pop.

A worker at a bottling company adds an ingredient to a batch of soda pop. Each company's exact recipes are kept secret.

When the bottles of flavor concentrate arrive at the bottling company, they go into the syrup room, where tanks of corn syrup are stored. The corn syrup and water are pumped into a big mixing tank. Together they make a simple syrup that will be mixed with the flavor concentrate.

After the simple syrup is pumped into another mixing tank, the flavor concentrate is poured in. A powder—citric or phosphoric acid—is added too. The acid gives soda pop its tangy taste. A propeller in the bottom of the tank stirs the ingredients. The mixture is called finished syrup.

In a section of the syrup room called the quality control lab, people test the finished syrup. They check the syrup under a microscope to make sure it doesn't contain germs. It probably won't. Soda pop factories are very careful to wash their equipment with boiling water and chemicals. The syrup must be checked every half hour—that's a law.

After being approved by the quality control lab, the finished syrup is pumped to the flow-mix machine. A flow-mix machine consists of three small tanks: one holds purified water, one holds finished syrup, and the other is for mixing the two together. About one part syrup is used for every five to seven parts water. The exact amounts depend on the flavor being made—and the recipe.

Once the syrup and water are mixed, it's soda pop without bubbles—and it's ready to be carbonated.

● Stacked one on top of another, the soda pop cans Americans use in one year would reach to the moon and back 10½ times. So please recycle your soda pop cans!

● Cola, ginger ale, and club soda have more bubbles in them than other kinds of soda pop. Orange sodas usually have the fewest bubbles.

Carbonation

There's no soda in the soda pop you drink. But people used to make the bubbles in beverages with soda and a mild acid. That's why soft drinks are called *soda*. The word *pop* comes from the sound a bottle or can makes when it's opened.

The bubbles in the soda pop you drink come from carbon dioxide—a colorless, odorless, tasteless gas. Carbon dioxide is created in a chemical process known as **fermentation.** Fermentation happens when bacteria, molds, or yeast break down certain substances, such as sugar. When yeast is added to bread dough, for instance, it creates carbon dioxide bubbles like the bubbles in soda pop. Without carbon dioxide, bread would be like a cracker—hard and flat.

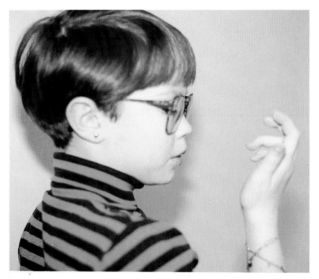

Blow on your hand. You've just created carbon dioxide. All animals make carbon dioxide when they exhale. A chemical process called fermentation creates carbon dioxide too.

With the following experiment, you can create enough carbon dioxide to inflate a balloon.

Equipment:

An empty 8- to 16-oz. bottle, either plastic or glass, with a narrow neck (remove label)
A balloon
A measuring cup

Ingredients:

3 packages of active yeast
1/4 cup sugar
1/2 cup warm water

Pour the ingredients into the bottle and mix well. Fit the balloon snugly over the bottle's neck. Shake gently. In about five minutes, the balloon will begin to inflate. You'll see a froth of tiny bubbles form in the bottle. This happens because carbon dioxide is being created from fermentation. The yeast is breaking down the sugar.

Inside the carbo-cooler, the carbon dioxide meets the sweetened, flavored water.

Many companies that manufacture corn syrup produce carbon dioxide as well. They make it by fermenting corn, and then they trap it—just like you did in the experiment on the opposite page.

The trapped carbon dioxide is forced into a tank, which compresses it, or squeezes it together. Then the compressed carbon dioxide is cooled. As it cools, the carbon dioxide turns into a liquid, which is then purified. Extra moisture is removed, along with anything else that is not carbon dioxide. Then it's piped into a storage tank or into a truck that goes to the bottling company.

When the carbon dioxide truck arrives at the bottling company, the driver attaches a hose to the truck's tank. The other end of the hose is connected to a tank at the factory.

The carbon dioxide is piped into a carbo-cooler, a big round refrigerator. Then the sweetened and flavored water is sprayed into the carbo-cooler too. As it enters the tank, the water absorbs the carbon dioxide gas. The cold, bubbly liquid can finally be called soda pop, and it's ready to be bottled and canned.

This worker is loading small tanks of carbon dioxide onto a truck, to be delivered to restaurants. Many restaurants and movie theaters buy carbon dioxide and flavor syrups separately. Then they mix fresh soda pop on the spot.

Canning and Bottling

One of the first things you would see if you walked into a bottling company is stacks and stacks of bottles and cans. The stacks almost reach the ceiling. If you examined one of the cans, you'd notice something strange. It doesn't have a top. The tops of the cans are nearby —packed in long paper rolls, like stacks of crackers.

A machine called a depalletizer places the cans on a conveyor belt that is similar to the moving belt at a supermarket checkout counter. In a factory, a conveyor belt moves things around from place to place, and from room to room.

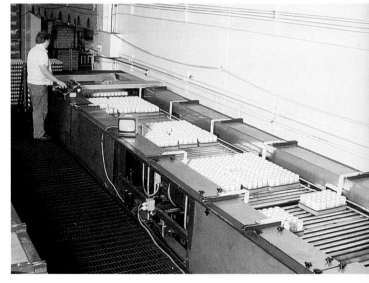

Cans traveling on a conveyor belt

First the cans travel to a rinser. Water sprays the cans inside and out. Then they enter the room with the carbo-cooler. This is where the cans will be filled.

A filling machine looks something like a merry-go-round. In the center is a big bowl, filled with fresh soda pop straight from the carbo-cooler. All around the filler bowl are round metal platforms. Above them are metal screws called heads. Each head has a tube attached.

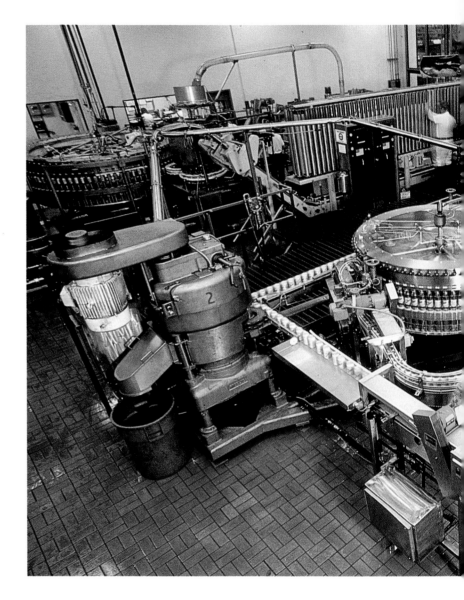

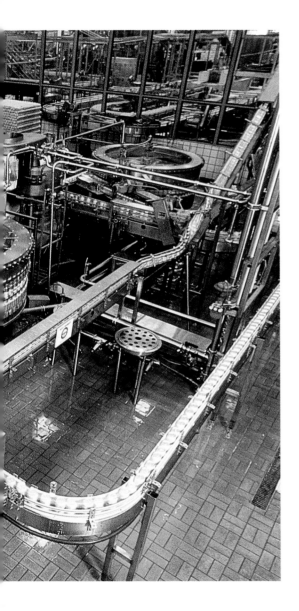

Left: *A conveyor belt transports cans to and from the filling machine.* Below: *Cans just filled with bubbly soda pop.*

A conveyor belt moves each can onto a platform. Each can is automatically attached to a head. The platform rises, and the tube squirts soda pop into the can. The cans immediately leave the filler to go to another machine called the capper.

Not all soda pop is canned. Another filler squirts soda pop into large plastic bottles.

From above the capper, the caps roll down a chute and meet the filled cans. A machine presses the caps on and folds the sides down. This all happens in less than a second. It has to happen this fast, otherwise bubbles will escape from the soda pop and the drink will taste flat.

The soda pop has now been canned, but it is not ready to be boxed yet. Just think how cold the cans have become—they're filled with near-freezing liquid. When you take a can or bottle of soda pop out of the refrigerator, it becomes damp. The same thing happens to the cans at the factory. If they were packed into cartons while still cold, they would become warm and damp inside the boxes. The boxes would get wet and fall apart. So the cans are warmed before they are boxed.

The can warmer works sort of like a car wash, as it sprays warm water on the cans. The cans dry very quickly and are then almost ready to be packed. But first the cans must go through another machine to be x-rayed to make sure they are full. If one is not full, a tiny electronic arm pushes the can off the conveyor belt. These cans won't be packed and sold with the others. The bottling company gives them to employees or sells them at a discount.

Now some of the cans are packed into boxes. The cans pass over flattened boxes and a machine pushes the sides of the boxes up. Glue is sprayed on the corners to hold the boxes together. Each box holds 12 or 24 cans.

Top: *Steam rises as warm water is sprayed over the cans.*
Bottom: *Packing cans into boxes.*

Bottling companies sell single cans of soda pop too. They're ready to be delivered to a store near you!

If the cans are to be put into six-packs, the conveyor belt lines them up in pairs. The cans move under a wide piece of plastic tape, which comes off a big roll. The tape has holes in it that are the size of a pop can. The tape drops over each set of six-cans and hooks them together.

The cartons or six packs are then stacked on a wooden frame called a pallet so that they can easily be moved around. A machine called a forklift lifts the pallets and takes them to a shipping area. The cases of pop are loaded onto a truck.

The soda pop is finally on its way to stores to be put on the shelves. Soon, you'll buy a can and pull open the metal tab. You'll hear the familiar popping sound and take a refreshing gulp.

1 Fun with Soda Pop

You can make your own soda pop at home. It won't taste exactly like the kind from the store, but it will taste good.

For two of the following recipes, you can create the bubbles yourself. The citric acid in orange and lemon juice reacts with the baking soda to produce carbon dioxide bubbles.

For each recipe, you will need a glass that holds 12 ounces or more. (If your glass is smaller, your drink will fizz over the top!) You will also need a measuring cup for liquids, measuring spoons, and a spoon for stirring.

FIZZY ORANGE SODA POP

6 ounces cold unsweetened orange juice
2 ounces cold water
3 teaspoons sugar or corn syrup, or a
   comparable amount of an artificial
   sweetener
1 teaspoon baking soda

Pour the orange juice and water into a
glass. Add the sugar and baking soda.
Stir. Almost immediately your drink
will fizz.

LEMON SODA POP

Juice of one lemon
8 teaspoons sugar or corn syrup, or a
   comparable amount of artificial
   sweetener
8 ounces very cold water
1 teaspoon baking soda

Squeeze the juice from the lemon into
a glass. Mix in the sugar and water. Add
baking soda last, and stir.

UNCOLA COLA

8 ounces cold club soda

Coloring:

4 drops yellow food coloring
2 drops red food coloring
2 drops blue food coloring

Flavor syrup:

1 teaspoon vanilla extract
1 teaspoon lemon juice
3 drops lime juice
1/4 teaspoon orange juice or orange extract
  (Extract is stronger and will give you a better flavor.)
Dash of nutmeg
Dash of cinnamon
8 teaspoons sugar or corn syrup, or a comparable amount of artificial sweetener

Put coloring ingredients in an 8-ounce glass. Mix until you have a nice caramel color—like cola. If the color looks a little green, add another drop of red coloring. Mix flavor syrup ingredients into the color mixture. Fill the glass with club soda. It tastes a lot like cola, doesn't it?

BOSTON COOLER, BLACK COW, or ROOT BEER FLOAT

1 12-ounce glass root beer
1 big scoop vanilla ice cream

Pour root beer into a glass. Drop in the ice cream. You'll get a nice fizz. This concoction is also delicious with strawberry soda pop or cola.

CHOCOLATE PHOSPHATE or EGG CREAM

3 tablespoons milk
1/4 cup chocolate syrup
12 ounces cold club soda

Mix the milk and chocolate syrup in the bottom of a glass. Pour in club soda.

METRIC CONVERSION CHART

WHEN YOU KNOW:	MULTIPLY BY:	TO FIND:
AREA		
acres	.41	hectares
LENGTH		
inches	25.00	millimeters
inches	2.54	centimeters
feet	30.00	centimeters
feet	.30	meters
yards	.91	meters
miles	1.61	kilometers
VOLUME		
teaspoons	5.00	milliliters
tablespoons	15.00	milliliters
fluid ounces	30.00	milliliters
cups	0.24	liters
pints	0.47	liters
quarts	0.95	liters
gallons	3.80	liters
WEIGHT		
ounces	28.00	grams
pounds	0.45	kilograms
tons	0.91	metric tons
TEMPERATURE		
Fahrenheit temperature	5/9 (after subtracting 32)	Celsius temperature

GLOSSARY

amino acids: The building blocks of protein. There are 20 amino acids in all, and they combine to form thousands of different proteins.

aspartame: An artificial substance made of two amino acids—phenylalanine and aspartic acid. Aspartame is used as a sweetener in soda pop.

bacteria: Living things that have only one cell and are so small that they can be seen only with a microscope. Some types of bacteria cause diseases.

calories: Units of measurement that measure the energy food supplies to the body.

carbonation: Bubbles in a liquid that are formed by carbon dioxide.

concentrate: A strong solution from which water has been evaporated.

dextrose: A type of sugar found in plants and animals; also called glucose.

enzyme: A substance that causes a chemical change in another substance but is not changed itself.

fermentation: A chemical change that takes place in a substance by means of bacteria, molds, or yeast. Fermentation creates carbon dioxide.

fructose: A type of sugar found in fruits and vegetables.

saccharin: An artificial sweetener sometimes used in soda pop.

starch: A white powdery substance found in the living cells of most plants, especially in potatoes, beans, and grains, such as corn.

sucrose: A type of sugar found in sugarcane and sugar beets.

INDEX

ACKNOWLEDGMENTS

This book would not have been possible without the generous help of the following people:

Mr. Mike Adanamy, The Royal Crown Bottling Company; Mr. Jim Rook, Sr., The Kemmerer Bottling Company; Ms. Susan Mann, Staff Attorney, Dr Pepper/Seven-Up Company; Mr. John J. McKenna, Liquid Carbonic Carbon Dioxide Corporation; Ms. Andrea Pokryfke and Mr. Andy Harder, AirCo Industrial Gases; Ms. Mary Jane Buehne, Technical Services Manager, Sweeteners, American Maize Products; Mr. William Ducey, Director of Sweetener Sales, American Maize Products; The National Soft Drink Association; Mr. Rick Ray, Global Aromatics, Inc.; Mr. Dan Riley, Customer Service Manager, Sweetener Business Group, A. E. Staley Manufacturing Company; Mr. Alan W. Buck, Archer Daniels Midlands Corporation; Ms. Kaye Patterson, Coca-Cola USA; the NutraSweet Company; and the Water Department of the City of Chicago.

"Coca-Cola" and the Dynamic Ribbon device are registered trademarks of The Coca-Cola Company and are used with permission.

The photographs in this book are reproduced through the courtesy of:

pp. 2, 33, 34, 35, Crown Cork and Seal Company, Inc.; p. 6, copyright 1987 John Madere; pp. 8, 23, 26, 29, 30, Kathy Raskob/IPS; p. 9, American Water Works Association; pp. 13, 27, 36, The Coca-Cola Company; pp. 16, 17, 19, 20, Cargill, Inc.; p. 18, Corn Refiners Association; p. 21, The NutraSweet Company; p. 24, Universal Flavor Corporation, a subsidiary of Universal Foods Corporation; p. 25, American Spice Trade Association; pp. 31, 37 (top), Cloud Kiss Beverage; pp. 32, 38, The Pepsi-Cola Company; p. 37 (bottom), Crystal Soda Water Company.

Front cover photograph courtesy of Crown Cork and Seal Company, Inc.
Back cover photograph by Karen Sirvaitis.

The publisher would like to thank Natalie Lund, John Murphy, Joseph Murphy, Ted Seykora, and Ty Thompson.

ABOUT THE AUTHOR

Arlene Erlbach has written more than a dozen books of fiction and nonfiction for young people. In addition to being an author, she is an elementary school teacher. She loves to encourage children to read and write, and she is in charge of her school's Young Authors' program. Ms. Erlbach lives in Morton Grove, Illinois, with her husband, her son, a collie, and three cats.